P9-CJF-532
04273314

Hordes of Writing

Also by Chus Pato:

In Galician:
Urania
Heloísa
Fascinio
A ponte das poldras
Nínive
Heloísa
m-Talá
Charenton
Hordas de escritura
Secesión

In Galician and Spanish:
Un Ganges de palabras
    (selected poems edited and translated by Iris Cochón)

In English:
Charenton
m-Talá

Also by Erín Moure:

Empire, York Street
Wanted Alive
Domestic Fuel
Furious
WSW (West South West)
Sheepish Beauty, Civilian Love
The Green Word: Selected Poems 1973–1992
Search Procedures
Pillage Laud
A Frame of the Book
O Cidadán
Little Theatres
O Cadoiro
Expeditions of a Chimæra (with Oana Avasilichioaei)
O Resplandor

OKANAGAN COLLEGE
LIBRARY
BRITISH COLUMBIA

CHUS PATO

Hordes of Writing

translated from Galician by
Erín Moure

Shearsman Books & BuschekBooks
Exeter   Ottawa

First published in the United Kingdom in 2011 by
Shearsman Books Ltd
58 Velwell Road
Exeter EX4 4LD   www.shearsman.com

ISBN 978-1-84861-167-2

and in Canada by
BuschekBooks
P O Box 74053
Ottawa, Ontario K1M 2H9   www.buschekbooks.com

ISBN 978-1-894543-68-2

Original text copyright © María Xesús Pato Díaz, 2008;
copyright © Edicións Galaxia, S.A., 2008.
Translations copyright © Erín Moure, 2011.

The right of Chus Pato, to be identified as the author, and Erín Moure
to be identified as the translator of this work has been asserted by them
in accordance with the Copyrights, Designs and Patents Act of 1988.
All rights reserved.

*Cover design by Erín Moure, incorporating a photograph of the Edificio Viacambre
in Ourense, Galicia, by Oana Avasilichioaei, 2007.
Author photo (page 89) copyright © Andrea Costas*

Library and Archives Canada Cataloguing in Publication

Pato, Chus, 1955-
    Hordes of Writing / Chus Pato ; translated from Galician
    by Erín Moure.

Translation of: Hordas de escritura.
Poems.
ISBN 978-1-894543-68-2

    I. Mouré, Erin, 1955- II. Title.

PQ9469.2.P37H6713 2011   869.1'4   C2011-902662-7

HORDES OF WRITING

Animality and Language

To bring Chus Pato's words into English, the translator must travel at breakneck speed, trying not to trip over tree roots and go flying. I still end up with skinned knees. Pato topples all lyric convention, and in a rush of grammatical and visual leaps, brings us face to face (kiss or collide!) with the traumas and migrations of Western Europe, with writing itself, and the possibility (or not) of poetry accounting for our animal selves: our selves who will die. The urgency of her task is such that Pato wriggles out of any known form of the poem, and out of the confines of the book. The poems translated here are those of *Hordes of Writing*, the third volume in her projected pentalogy *Method*, in which she refashions the way we think of the possibilities of poetic text, of words, bodies, political and literary space, and of the construction of ourselves as individual, community, nation, world.

"I wanted to write a book that did not derive its structural unity from free verse, but from a horde of words: a protective mechanism borne deep inside it, but with maximum freedom, and mobility," says Pato. "The horde is the perfect mode of human relation because it is the perfect protective space for human beings, like the mother's womb. It also makes us think of constant movement, of mobility like the barbarians had, with their absolute freedom."

Chus Pato comes from a very literate culture (think of the riches of the medieval *cantigas*), albeit one small in numbers, that flourishes despite being under siege, yet it passes almost unperceived by readers in English. I think it critical to my own culture to bring discomfiting—and exhilarating—work such as Pato's into Canadian literature, into literature in English, to perturb us and upend our views of writing's possibilities.

Her work returns freedom to us, not that of the individual speaking from an illusory autonomy constructed on the invisibility of others, but the freedom to be organism among others and receive others as organisms, migrants, blastulæ, lives. "The poet is he or she whose muse has been integrally destroyed," writes Pato.

But there is always a remnant, she says, and from this remnant the poet picks up the pen again, and keeps writing.

"Rather than letting the world into my writing," says Pato, "I kick writing out into the world." Her works—such shock mechanisms—have made her one of the most revered and iconoclastic figures in Galician literature.

Erín Moure
September 2010

for Manuel

Position yourself in front of the narrowest

now veer 180 degrees
then the granite dilates and you're born (this word of blood)
head first, like Lenz, on January 20, in the mountains

**

now you and I (linguistic mammals) are here, on this stony bench,
because you wanted to show me this tree under which Friar
Martiño held his *Colloquium of 24 Rustic Galicians*

from close up the treetop is circular, spongiform, and the trunk an
umbilical cord that links us acoustically to the core of the planet

we transmigrate to a branch, like twins, so that we'll be oak or
placenta, which means we're in the midst of it[1] or *La connaissance
infinie*

***

a birth is a republic of trees

[1] It wasn't uncommon to mummify the pharaoh's placenta after birth,
keeping it forever as talisman . . . The ancient Egyptian custom of bearing the
placenta before the sovereign in processions existed from the 4th millennium
BCE up to the age of the Ptolemys: from it came later cults of veneration
of the flag.

Poetry is a republican discourse: speech that is its own law and own purpose, and in which all parts are free citizens who have the right to speak their minds so as to come to agreement.

FRIEDRICH SCHLEGEL

Thermidor
(first episode)

[▪]

Let's start with (Hrg) at the bus stop with a bag of animalcule

reason finds nothing strange in this snapshot; the protagonist does what she always does, only this time she has to cover a distance of 2000 kilometres, which isn't so rare either

(the green slate floor of the airport in the country where it always rains)

and she stands up as hero, as multitude, as protagonist, any episode that unites us

[▪]

It's best to sleep with the window open, rocked by wind and the torrential mix of every water, or on high peaks, or on the banks of the great fluvial arteries of her continent and with them (the arteries) on the sled of one of her woman ancestors she crossed the Rhine, frozen, and continued on foot along Imperial trails toward the country of great forests // heading always toward the purple of sunset, from the Black Forest over the pass from the Jura to the Vosges, the wide Saône plain, fertile fields of Champagne and Poitou (Jurassic), the region of the Landes or the cradle of Aquitaine (Tertiary), the icy passes of the Pyrenees, the Cretaceous nation of the Basques, the Cantabrian cordillera and the Navia River

—when will you write of the Suevi people meeting the hero or heroine . . . ?

—I decide that the heroine meets some historical figure, I decide this so as to extend the time of narration, confuse it, make it real. In this case the difficulty lies in choosing the figure, finally I make it a collective exodus: I'm interested in describing the itinerary. There's no vision, no voice; if there were it'd detail ice and waters flowing in the earth's core, the whiteness of the horizon, blue of the sky, the pelts, weapons, horses, the cold and this strange adventuress who's welcomed as family, the contrast between Germanic voices and the protagonist's language. And so on. Once decided, the rest is force, propulsion, perception and commotion, womb and logic of language

the heroine imagines a round thatched house with a single space for meals, work and love and falls asleep exhausted and her body scarcely touches the planet

—do all girls play games of recovery from ecological disasters?
—some do
(reader / author-she)
—they all have toy bathyscaphes?
—not all, some do

[■]

Not even her continual transit, this perpetual state of passage: all sorts of signs, feelings, messages, whatever

like the monstrous face of freedom, that slalom of abysses

[■]

A penchant for rest that manifests in a slowing of mental processes and relaxation of the body until images of terrestrial harmony flow, thus forests (and always, always, oak woods that derive unclassifiable pleasure from the damp soil, grey clarity of the skies or scant solar rays), plus ocean (and always, always, the Atlantic) and coastline: sands, dunes, marine birds but also—halfway between the surface of the waters and the abysmal deeps—images of submersion that invariably bring her to her double placenta which in the months of her own gestation allowed her to develop the requisite organs for what she identifies as "origin": the passion for walking, and language. Sometimes in these navigations she visualizes her daughters and through this watery flood she enters in lamination with all the nutritive forces of the species, because of this, enunciation always, always reiterates a rhythm // sanguine

time, anyone's or nobody's // an elevated consumption of words

[■]

It hits her right in mid-crosswalk, after deciding to walk from bus stop to hotel, she realizes she's too laden with baggage; and when she showers, the water gives her lovely curls and after getting ready for a first meeting she told herself that not only was she all primped and glowing but she's far more stunning now than in her youth and soon she walks the sidewalk as if she never, never daydreams and she realizes how much she'd like it if she were with Antón Lopo right now that she is the happiest protagonist of a novel on earth and she doesn't think at all of nausea

—and then?

—Marta and Publio arrived but Marcelo had to go defend the Austro-Hungarian border

[■]

Thus years went by—she said—and the need for verbal communication lost ground to an automatic proliferation of corporeal symptoms: lakes, vertigo, disorientation, disinterest she herself noticed and even, speaking as a woman who, feeling violated, finds strength to speak and emits words close to a language of madness and even uses an inconclusive scriptural protocol in which no term is arrived at with pleasure but only with exhaustion or fatigue and in this retreat of the voice she felt progressively closer to a vaporization of presence or headed definitively to an ending or notion of death

(…) curiously and despite it all, the reason for her wanderings was simple proximity to certain artworks; these almost never provoked emotion in her (I recall her in Munich impassive in front of Altdorfer's *Battle of Alexander at Issus*). It was never the experience of Cezanne's painting that moved her but the direct sight of the Montagne Sainte Victoire and the painter's effort faced with this mountain, faced with the canvas, and Cezanne striding back and forth, over and over, under scorching mountain light and that final encounter of the painter with the mountain and the final syncope. The mountain and its direct contemplation at dawn, from a service station on the ten-lane motorway in Provence, headed to Marseilles or Monaco

delirium is public and triple: a photographer, a painter and an older writer. Shoeless and sleepy I ask what they're doing there:

the painter drapes a blanket over my shoulders, I wrap my arms around his neck in a sign of infantile-erotic submission and he brings me back to bed. Around 3 p.m. we dine: by then the photographer had time to explain to the writer that the painter's relationship with me is the fruit of a violent and inadmissible passion that at its height involved attempted murder, regardless we kept on seeing each other in a state of exhaustion and extenuation joined to a kind of dementia or retreat of reason

abstraction, as you know—the photographer continued politely—can't be represented. This is what it means to him: an inconceivable state of intelligence, a current state of signs

[■]

The orange marble floors at the airport in the country where it hardly ever rains

[■]

For someone not very susceptible to suggestion, the illusion of bodily belonging, even for brief instants, was gratifying

she'd have liked to have dedicated a large part of her life to the cultivation of pleasure, which gave her the idea of setting up, in the way of the monks of Ménilmontant, Fourierist phalansteries or the city of *New Harmony*, utopian-revolutionary harems or bordellos where a community of women and men willingly reach the ideal of a phratria of bodies

in general the erotic scenes she imagined were the fruit of these *Weltanschauung*, thus the fling with an English aristocrat (she was presented in a circus cage and gilded with gift ribbon)

or with a 15th century gentleman in the Brabant (ergastulum, physiological splendour, torn clothing, gloom)

some people's judgments of Sade she found superfluous and banal, in her opinion the literary works of the Marquis (one of her bedtime favourites) could only be understood as another inventory and as the writer's attempt to make bearable the dark *night of the world*

her intelligence was ferocious, slow to accumulate (due to distraction, inattention and laziness) and avid toward language. She could anticipate the amorous struggle just by her response to a text, detect perfectly with which author/ess it would be possible, and if so who would win her over, who would conquer her and to whom she would surrender. Before a body or a piece of fiction her reaction was the same, so that it could be said that she didn't distinguish between body and writing

Cecilia, voice: Imperial dome

(an entire life at the barricades)

[■]

Generally in her youth she travelled and we can confirm she only lived in art galleries because these buildings lifted her spirits, and only did the food suit her there (especially at the Gulbenkian Foundation, the Tate or the small Vasarely collection). Today the spinning not only hadn't stopped, it had sped up and increased in amplitude but she had no way to get to a museum, exceptionally some accident might detain her in a city, thus Irish Iron-Age lunulas or peatbog mummies in the snowy city of Dublin

she greeted mobility as one facet of freedom and this made her a lucky protagonist, despite it being true that freedom is polyhedral and its facets and crevices innumerable. The weakness that attacked her from time to time, the forgetting of the rules of pugilism, was evidence of her ever growing need to go back or find a way to take cover

the storm space in Missolonghi when she was recovering from a fractured vertebra, her slow walk to the balcony and the palm trees and araucarias and thistle of Lord Byron, dead in the war against the Turks for Greek independence, and sarcophagus

—all this you're writing, is it true?
(and the author/she answered the reader, who is an infinity or two)
—it's a chronicle
—and if it were a poem?
—then it would speak of storm potential or time's acceleration

[■]

But nothing can be captured, not the ramification of open arteries, nor the volcano of incandescent lava, not even the perpetual glacier

nor any new form of basic life or colonization of moss or lichen . . .

hers was not a genuinely revolutionary temperament, rather rebellious and loyal, engrossed in a scar that healed only slowly //

this fake lock as atmosphere // solitary childhood among the less favoured, from whom she was separated only by the thinnest of membranes cast by her father to protect her, especially among her schoolmates who with time's passage swelled the lines of desolation and emigration to the British Isles and central Europe

the absence of fascist protection in her family, time spent in the ancestral village, and a certain type of intelligence able to tell lies from truth had conditioned Hrg's later decision, and thus it was always impossible for her to relinquish the idea that private ownership of the means of production was not only corrupt and immoral but abominable, this and her belief in the radical equality of all human beings

all this fuelled her revolutionary activities which you can't exactly say she chose, but that she found it impossible to dislodge them from her path

from the past, from her childhood, she maintained certain friendships and a clandestine but ongoing presence in murky dives like *The Little Red Lighthouse* or *Tabanaco*, or even more dubious and recondite dumps: the *Suevia* or the *Paradise*

or her never fatal attraction to her currently uprooted, jailed or dead comrades

so it was, in the stony native city of the author

in which Ophelia was brutally run over when she tried to identify her brother amid the corpses of the victims of the latest bombardment

[■]

I trace a meridian: north and south
it's me (arms held at my sides). My horizontal abscissa is a starry
equator

head: huge houses for eternity: our position here is to reach an
inner nucleus of earth
corridor of wee granite ancestral idols: Dombate
it's true you sleep on your heart (childhood)

womb: pale // all the chambers of writing

my desire is Jekyll, a romantic-sublime animal; his first habitat is
the dissection cabinets, the flasks of blood

nadir: the only possible mode of habitation and deterioration is
the empire of the wind (body)

**

But today reading the essay 'Figures, Doors and Corridors' by
Robin Evans (Ilford, Essex 1944—London 1993) and, especially,
seeing the photo of the United Nations in it, I note the impossibility
of all architecture, as Evans predicts: an end to the architectonic
project of modernity now that the greater part of the population
live in refugee camps

the article first appeared in *Architectural Design*, Vol. 48, No.
4, April 1978 and since then the process has not only failed to
subside but is more generalized every minute, more anguished and
extensive

I read that Evans article in Galician translation in the second issue of *Os monografías, revista de arte e arquitectura*, published with support from the Galician Architects Association, dedicated to THE ROOM. I wrote the preceding text for this issue. You'll note that the person who defines herself therein can be described as dismissed, expulsed or hurled practically off the planet, held to it only by gravity and the equator as sole point of contact. The head can imagine itself as already in astral space along with the stony interments of prehistory, plus the heart and chambers of writing, and pails of blood too: she'd be leaning precipitously outward, with only her nadir (feet) touching the muck of earth, as when we lean over a balcony for a better view

[■]

I see her again at the bus stop and she's flustered because she wants to stub her cigarette where she's supposed to, beside the bus shelter, and ends up crushing it on the sidewalk: pointless. Finally she's on the bus and contemplates the city but not the part where she used to live, an industrial area abandoned even then, and she wonders if its magnificent brick chimneys are still standing

"I can't remember when I arrived, when I truly got there, nor if I was ever there before this "when I arrived"; I can see another departure with a backpack full of tins and, how I'd fallen in love with a stranger, the house we'd share in the industrial zone, an intermission in Milan station and the explosion of desire; before that, the rendezvous in a café that could only exist in a Mediterranean dictatorship: I'd arrived from the north, he from Florence, Milan, Venice . . . no, even better: Naples"

(Hrg, monologue)

[■]

"I went in and the roofs of the old warehouse refurbished as
library soared up and the walls ended in an octagonal tower,
profusely decorated with shells and Nasrite honeycomb; I went to
find whoever'd let me in and ended up in a very spartan sacristy
that opened onto slaughterhouses: a bunch of people arrived with
a burro and the burro carried octopus and other marine species
and everyone dined and a woman urged me to share the vomit of
the animal, and beyond a doubt this was one of the dungeons or
calabooses of silence"

(Hrg, vision)

[■]

Silence can't be seen: we walk in fields of greener grass and below,
in the tangle or lineage of roots, silence spreads out (of all of you,
who still believe in the power of great narratives and affirm the
existence of sacred texts, I'll say nothing; we are your bridge and
feel your weight in each vulnerable vertebra // because we don't
want to die

we're on the other side // five thousand dead men and women of
the free Commune of Paris, we are // those destroyed in the prisons
of the tropical Guayanas and it all comes back to the beginning
again and we would like to live

the house we share and where we visit you is another cell of terror:
nothing's sacred where we are, not even blood, nothing)

"silence when I type into the computer and jellyfish and dragonflies flit across the screen, or when from the treasures I rescue the presence of friendship and realized that I fought back from the start—and violently—throwing quicklime and more gobs of quicklime at the wall to ensure no one sees the holes or end of such suffocating narrative

from here error is visible and acceptable, and the cracks irreparable"

(Hrg, monologue)

[■]

we (wildflowers) occupy the barrens and for us the sparse vegetation that breathes with difficulty and fragility between the cracks and holes of the infernos is constitutive

[■]

Silence is a medium and allows her to immerse herself in clarity and voice and apparitions from the past, as well as intervene in the present. Silence as womb of a detention, of a wordless dwelling that permits understanding, bringing and carrying off absences, uttering words that will never again be utterable

What most resembles silence on this trip are the dreams of Hrg, mute, dreams almost no one speaks of, induced or chemical and almost always altered; in the hotel, in Cecilia's bedroom, in the bed of the country where it always rains

[■]

Maybe the biggest silence is me (the narrator, she), a solitary thinking voice that never addresses anyone. Reader, will you read my enchained body, pomegranate or lyrics out loud? recite to me in your voice? ink, shadow of grain or perhaps a husband of mine, Hades, in the foggy cellars of the planet

and Hrg, who'll never speak either, though her conversations and memories exist in themselves and all the answers and questions of this chronicle are yours, dear reader, or those of whoever will sign this text with a fictitious name

(the contract stipulates twenty pages, but no directive on the excellence of those pages)

Thebes: (continuation)

The dreams of Mariana (Hrg) are short, not very restorative, and superficial. An eloquent voice tries to interest her in its story: it talks to a dead woman, to a stone

Jekyll's on a poetry jury; when the originals arrive he realizes he authored one of the books; in starting to read it he sees that it's not his words and none of its texts were written by him[1]

---

[1] that's not true, Jekyll goes down the stairs (he lives on the fourth floor at 48 Havana Street) and heads off on his daily stroll: he takes Cardenal Quevedo Street, heads into Santo Domingo, arrives at Iron Square where he loiters in front of the baroque fountain dragged from the monastery at Oseira (here he stops to doff the blue raincoat inherited from his late father) and continues on Peace Street, crossing Main or Magdalena to emerge at the Posío Gardens; in fact, he repeats over and over the same itinerary of his childhood walks with his progenitor to visit birds, wisteria and lindens and palm trees at the edge of his native city, experience that culminates in utter astonishment at the spread tailfans of the two male examples of the peacock that offer themselves motionless to his gaze in the gardens

(input from the police commissioner)[2]

---

[2] fog today with hard gusts from the south, almost gale-force. I head anyway down to the Catalan pier and dawdle in the ruins of the tide mill and in contemplating the estuary, cross the bridge and walk nearly to Serres: I barely pause to admire the navelwort flowering in the stone walls and the remains of boats rotting in the puddles. I return past the marble quarry and the textile cooperative, not without first recalling the sad image of prisoners of war kept in intolerable conditions in the building, today decrepit, that was the fish saltery, turned into a concentration or extermination camp

(Jekyll, notes in his diary)

Mariana, in terror, reads the news in the paper, goes digging for diaries and agendas, realizes that on November 3 she was in the Caribbean and couldn't possibly have chaired the "Friends of the Nation" committee that refused to commission a pedestal or high relief to the victorious armies as a trophy or booty. Even so, someone who looked so much like her that she could have passed for her had chaired the jury

In the desolation of a moonless night, she contemplates the pedestal or high relief in detail. On it a very young woman guides an old blind man and points out or explains or leads him to a new city that, she intuits, is not in the mosaic: in the leafy treetop Jekyll learns the language of birds

she abandons the square and heads to the *creepy passage*, to tunnels shaped like helicoidal sheep's horns, stuck into the thicket where Jekyll lives

—so, could it be said that Mariana heard the lament of God in the throes of death?
—yes, the voice of Jekyll

—does this mean Mariana's genealogy is of divine origin?
—(?)

Jekyll's office is an "anatomy lesson," as such, the most recondite foyer of the maternal body is crammed with gentlemen seated on benches, a coroner and a corpse

In the ergastula, chained and practically immobile, the female loveslaves, Mariana's infinite replicas, await the call to artfully pleasure their solicitous lovers: today in a commotion they break out, bursting from the subterranean galleries or sewers and, like lionesses in heat, or better, rhizomes of doe ermines, they leap to the surface

Mariana on the tundra feels them coming and faints, not without first recalling the baptismal sprinkling of bull's blood in the brotherhood of adepts of Mithras

on the verge of catastrophic hallucination

She'd never thought of it that way, as a leaning building, but they all leaned. No street was straight and you couldn't say any of them, even those opened up in the 60s, offered a view; maybe from this intersection: a sort of rapid plunge before being boxed in by sunset, but the direction wasn't right for it ended in the small valley of the tributary; the main river was deep and full but not wide enough and wasn't visible from anywhere. So we'd never realized it, but before there were houses and streets, it was a riperian landscape, a double bowl configured by both rivers and it wasn't hard to imagine all sorts of aquatic vegetation and a temperate climate, as the row of cork trees indicated.

Mariana's life was limited to a street cut in two: south from the intersection it was all stone, buildings dating mostly from the 19th, ending in a square, also granite, centred on a baroque fountain. North of the intersection it was still stone, but built in the first 36 years of the 20th. At the end was the park or ground where the cattle market had been held; since then the oaks were felled, and palm trees planted for shade and, as well, to the west and centre of the square rose a colossal monument to The Fallen. Mariana spent hours trying to climb this statue and when she did she felt dizzy, as if it were too hot or she were overdressed, or just in a daze; it wasn't clear and she couldn't put her finger on it, just as with nearly everything that happened to her. This west stretch was that of defeat.

Across from her house rose the Finance Ministry, a building very much in the corporatist style of the dictatorship of 1923, with impressive columns and two civil guards to protect it.

Mariana didn't ask questions: she dashed down the stairs, walked seven doors down and entered the school. The classroom, as she remembers it, was so chaotic she could lose herself perfectly there and pass unnoticed; she often slipped out to the patio and inspected the latrines. Mariana's doorway was trimmed in Maghrebi tiles.

She'd been baptized in one of the chapels of St. Euphemia of the North. At some point she realized that in this building, at certain times she couldn't pinpoint, it was possible to let something float that was nameless but definitely inside her; consequently she was given to visiting not only this church but also the small Paulist chapel; naturally, being a teenager, she'd have noted the towering cathedral (also stone)

just west of this and parallel to it was the Falangist Street of Sundays

there were names with no geography: Loña, Rabaza, Ceboliña, and the mythical Buenos Aires Avenue that she just knew the start of.

After grade school her parents moved temporarily while they awaited a new house in the street that would later be named after Valle Inclán and was now just a muddy track; from this seventh floor apartment Mariana began a perfect daily circle: up Bedoia, cross Buenos Aires, continue on Bedoia to San Francisco, contemplate the gently glowing basin of the Miño and Barbaña rivers and go into school; on the way home, they went down San Francisco to Corrector Square (peering into the *Green Frog* and *Black Cat*), came out in Iron Square, walked down the Street of Sundays, reached the park, went up Bedoia, turned and took the elevator up the seven floors that separated her from her bedroom. Six years went by; on the seventh the circuit widened: at Iron Square she headed toward the Main Square on Liberty and across Vilar (the bars *Suevi, Paradise*) till reaching high school, from where she could see the Posío Gardens (…)

i

On the other side, where we're alone with time and *I* is an innumerable that multiplies and decentres itself

given that this narrator (of "Thermidor")—who still has no name and whose contract the author didn't renew as she's inadequate and inconsistent—couldn't permit herself the luxury of not being osmotic even though yes she wore a trench coat.

The account is autobiographical in that the words that form it are biography

ferocity writes naturalizing poetics; its torpour opiatic, geometric.

ii

Emotional tension runs high. She orders a shot of J&B. She volatizes (we find her by the shine of her boots, but her face blurs). Not even the most infinitesimal part of the tiniest bit of distance between her and her surroundings: guardians of the ambiguous, conversations and above all fusion with the black vessel that is really a theatre. Words, syntactic segments, reverberate in her eardrums, right to her gut. If what—cinematographic—she's now watching is a prosthesis of dream, what sort of technology is the poem?

iii

Because of him, Oedipus, his alabaster skin, his Nile-green eyes, his body hunched in the bulwarks, the sounds of his harmonica, she forgot her sworn faith in reason, belief in progress. It wasn't then that she learned the virtues of the dildo and the equivalence of bodies.

iv

And you, who can never fit together names and objects.

v

Since she can't remember, she takes notes. She glosses coagulations (on the skin).

Altai, Yablonovy, Stanovoy (mountains)
Darfur, Kimberley (plains)
Orinoco, Mekong (deltas)
Challenger (grave)
Ob, Yenisey, Amur, Huang He (rivers)

vi

And the delta, that tongue of earth, full of light, advances.

alpha.—

The cleft is conventional, a seismic movement of low intensity, in the synthetic pavement of a garden. Underground, the same fracture.

It's possible to fit lyrical-sanguine series into each segment of the opening (yellow fog that lifts light over snowy landscapes) or into each side of the three types of hexagonal lattice in the Central Place Theory of Christaller

nothing desires to be written

Hölderlin

Renaissance.

....

Once in a while the birds aren't scared of me
I'm almost part of the flock.

***

In the shade of 12 shrubs, an alder and three apple trees on a lawn twenty by eighty metres, at 3 p.m. 14 days before the spring equinox // the hours tick by. They reproduce the root.

In this snowbound winter in which the only possible dialogue is with the birds time, two-faced: a felicitous unfolding of bodies in space, the cold, the heron

the crack in the same sheet of grass

omega.—

the eyes are those of a dead woman, she writes // absorbed in the fracture
dream of a verse by Pondal

what she sees are all the cities sinking into the core of the planet and the seas

the fissure is a cataclysm spookily illuminated
Earth's double and shadow

its edges, a sprinkling of very pale ash

enlightened.

**

it's true that death is here a thick reversible wool overcoat

the flagstones are felt, grey with light streaks

and the most concentration on a discourse, that of the sleeping woman

....

the layer of algae is pain, it rolls in the waters // and light, its beauty

It's not that I believed that communication flows work according to Christaller's hierarchy, what fascinates me is imagining this spume enfolding the planet and plunging into its depths, and oceans pouring through the openings thus the NiFe (astral) would know the joy of whales

and the sandal of

Empedocles.

severity // talophytes

We Wish We Were Birds
and We Don't Like Binoculars

The voice was panic
and wanted, insisted on having its way in the poem
....

but not everything can be transported (not the voice, obviously)

yes *the spirit that invades the bard, between sharp briars*

and because it's raining, the poem's inhabitants have to open their
umbrellas // grab everything they brought in and run outside to
find shelter

[only because you've stuck your nose in the text can I proceed to
solutions]

this is what Mr. Amiable does, he makes alienated beings appear
in the world and, much to his regret, as free persons

but only the voice fills the three tales
the voice that writing doesn't cover

as such, a poet is an ancient being.

Instead of letting the world into the poem,
the poet kicks writing out, like a soft and transparent lava, muslin

all this sky
all this springtime

you see, this is a political act: wresting the will from all those who
obey

but without context.

And where to write it down!, for paper doesn't last and all that's imaginable is a wall and the digital projection of letters (clearly in a museum or on freeway signs) or those same phrases looping the bodies of travellers as if with luminous sashes as they dialogue on the flight of birds or the hovering of falcons that blend in with the trees when they spread their wings like a nest

Theory is that ethical violence of the intangible

and is the problem of the I, how many? and of situations

I prefer my panic on entering bookstores, leaving you behind, who abandon me everywhere, without money, or in the car with no handbrake. We visit a city to recall the edifices of cities

dreams are not theory, and now we're stuck here because you're loathe to wake up in this palace of privatized urbanization, alongside so many others whose condition we share. Tonight our murderers are drunk or shut in the toilet

once and for all, nothing hermetic, or cryptic (which we never write anyhow) and I send it into orbit, with all our splendid manures and heathers.

And do you notice how truth is sweeter when you linger shoeless, weightless?, in the placenta of alders

**

the synapses are back, the disturbing bursts of April flowers

Like many of her compatriots she'd been trained in anachoresis and delirium. *I* was an empty site, therefore *I* was a site that could only be substituted by affect: otherwise, *I* would be destroyed.

You burst in from meaning

you don't cover it over, you weave it
weave what you'll never be able to say
and weave it with ice, with human breath, with tree, river.

Signs are indifferent but dream and copulate
reason is slower
from the side that speaks we accumulate catastrophes

naturally we're in the garden, in a protected dimension, and all arts derived from light—painting, film and flesh—precede the voice. Thus writing would be composed of radical signifiers; our text'd stem from luminous processes, telefilms, dream and copulation. We'd all be quickly non-clothed, non-naked and our names instantaneously fit their subjects

the eyes, tired (blind) scarcely discern
dictate:

"(…) despite what many believe, no contiguity registers between poem and delirium, the latter shored up in a narrative structure. If you want a comparison, try sitcoms. A delirious subject starts off from an I (or less-I to be more exact) that won't link properly to any family romance, submitted to an extreme violence

the auras of delirium are glorious, incited to permanent resurrection, bodies of the apocalypse

any small rodent, under stress, is delirious.

Sex is a scene of light

thus what we call intimacy

are lips, really butterflies.

*

I is in the ice and in morning
I is in river mist and in morning

my name // in the tree.

The body
elastic, amiable

says no to everything that's not respiration but self-conscious, self-
reflexive, slow.

*

The kingdom never existed, barbarians didn't have to barge across
borders; but yes, yes, this: in the fortress lives the woman artist
with the bronze gaze; maybe she should trim the grass growing in
the roof tiles, or the wisteria, heavy in the south

in due time she, who lived with the most musical head in the
language, went on a trip: and there we were, in fields, in a huge
tantrum, at summer's end

All best to the quinces
to dogs and abandoned bitches
to the heron to come

really she has no silk-lined case (the question is unanswerable
because it'd denounce and betray me to eros like a mess of
loneliness) the colour of blood, violet and violent and clearly I lost:
like love which is a mom thing, a womb thing, of indiscriminate
spit, that leaks just like meaning

and I notice gold and those animals I love so much (my country—
she continued—is a collapsible wall, a double river of alphabetic
reading).

Okay now: glands don't speak; when induced to rapid secretion,
in times of closure, depopulation or movement, they just barely
invade the breath: the way a lover or imaginary gaze projects an

avalanche—heavenly—of global architectural-oxygen upon the flesh

let's call this dysfunction *unreal deployment* or *pituitary hallucination*

when these messengers rule the imagination, reason desertifies (any desert where camels perhaps gaze undomesticated): it's the pituitary talking

and she wanted, wanted badly, that the dissolution of her organs incarnate letters on dark and western soils, just like other animals, until they form a huge tomb at one of the furthest *earthly frontiers*. And the dangers of her unfounded art, oriented like lichen toward a chimærical writing of estrus, toward north (may everything she reads in books happen to her)

really what she has is a coffer of aches

and no scandal causes her the absence of basic significance

in this way and with all deals already scuttled, I'll have to make my own solstice—svelte.

I crumble in light, in a sfumato not at all baroque

(as nerves configure the leaf, the fractures pass through me)

animal *I*
drinks
thought and albumin

sprout by sprout, the fracture sustains what stares right at it

your thinking, so unlike mine, and my thinking
are made vulnerable by desire
are water or a sky

they cede as skin cedes, as the zipper before a body

they infiltrate

layers and more layers of oneiric thickness

unstable and stirred up like clouds of insects

The poem

functions stuporous and doesn't notice

we reject glaciers, lakes, tombs

each petal in its holder, alchemy or double

I myself trip the device that turns life into a clock

the girl.

Flowerings, of thought, of waters, of sky
absorb

like the scribble the vine makes against the wall

the incessant passage of the clouds
the nonexistent rain
the populous cities

I believe—she continued—that my sole interlocutor is death:
somehow I write so that death, whatever its circumstances, can't
be debased. As such, I write in common words, identical to those
anyone uses

(with you, inorganic
with all the dispersed salts
you were there, logos from the start)

in the dome and in the womb in the dome and in the womb
in the dome and in the womb in the dome and in the womb
in the dome and in the womb in the dome and in the womb
in the dome and in the womb in the dome and in the womb

and the fire of stars
in the womb

no, it's not stage fright, it's a shame hard to explain, the public
exhibition of this ruin

one ocean exists for the amoeba, another for the medusa, another
for *anemonia sulcata*; it's complicated and what's more I'm not at
ease, though I've no need to fear time

knowing you're a residue doesn't mean degradation, in fact it's the only way to survive, not because you'd prefer the way it was before which is at the same time a residue of what went before (and so on) but because it's not possible to restore that caesura

*

Definition: poet is the non poet

1st Proposition: the true poet is the one whose muse has been integrally destroyed

Scholium: if whoever writes poetry is the one whose muse was destroyed, this means that poet and non-poet are never perfectly identical, that it is not possible to integrally destroy the muse, a residue always remains. To be poet is to be that residue

(according to the geometric order)

(...) these waters coexist but are not identical, this indivisible intimacy

It's not so much the subject of her reading (*sovereignty is the zone of indifference between violence and law*) but its expositional form that affects the debate

it makes her glad

like mountains, trees, beauty.

The airfields again, baggage lost
as if she's stuck forever in a relation of belonging and non-inclusion on another continent

outside the flock
outside the flag

in a pack of she-wolves (abandoned), of she-bandits who are meaning, a revolver in each voice.

The indolent low-pressure zones in the S. Atlantic

the cubic waves
that's what they are (the father arrived years later, didn't know his grandchildren or how to work the DVD or any other home electronics)
a farmwoman who crosses the ocean and, a century later, writes.

In reality, at certain points of her life, she rereads the same book: a story of invariable versions about gods, omens and tombs; the sentences don't lead her onward, no faith exalts her

when she experiences amorous ecstasy, the violence of rapture—a constitutive violence vague as a snow squall, a swarm of bees or pale torchlight inundating gods, omens and tombs—thus pleasure—a far cave, dark fog, blue, ashen, grey as a Himalaya—she incises letters in the weft of papyrus

that grotto, its gloom and the sighs of pleasure articulate the power of what bursts from language

Like dough we roll out until it fills an entire geometry, like a tangle of sprouts

bodies are consistent, they establish meaning.

What I'm trying to clarify is that, despite its seminal configuration, the authorial incision can neither coincide with nor tend toward either of the two counterposed series. All in all, given that the poem only inscribes itself where its concretion is impossible (outside the archive or the already-recorded), it can't be faithful to any of the three described categories. Perhaps this is why insects, birds and certain mythological creatures (victories, cupids and the she-messenger of the gods, along with the angelic hierarchies) are winged.

Even though the previous text privileges the simile "a column of butterflies," the huge canyon dividing the banks of the Sil would also work, as would the scales of Osiris

(these three comparisons don't at all exhaust the topological analogies that illustrate the hypothesis)

** *Three lines of introduction in a colloquial register, for Krakow*

Look at it this way: over here, the impossibility of writing, over there, a power of writing (symmetrical like butterfly wings), in the middle, *I*: *I* is a fracture. The poem invents that which doesn't concur, is loyal only to its own independence and beauty.

(...) and thus I burned each and every manuscript after it was published. If my words had to circulate among their contemporaries, their bare life, their—to put it this way—intimate symbiosis with disappearance should be dissected and offered at summer solstice to the potentates of Averno, to Earth and to the gases that make existence possible

so that all I'd written could be considered as material that inhabits different worlds—she-wolf head –

This—she concluded—is the status or territory of a poet

poet is any human whatsoever.

Though lightning blinds some, others are blinded by the scar of night

—I have to think on it, what you call a deliberately schizo ego . . . But, hey, I started as distributed or bifurcated nuclei, where a split maintains and divides a siamese face, bifacial

so I see the *I* not exactly as a dislocation but as an argument that sustains the parts (the *I* would be the insect's quinine, the variable and undammable waters of the river, the scale's needle). On one hand the so-called "state of nature"; on the other, syntax, but both flow, one into the other

abyss that, as you well know, refers to the crack in the female sex, opening into fleshy lips

so different than the phallus that rises toward an infinite, supported by the dilation of blood vessels

the voices of this *I* would be a register that doesn't pass through the lungs, commonly known as mental words that start in the head then go through the chest without using the diaphragm, musical notation become woman, like a pure (English) countertenor voice

When head down you navigated the mother

like how, in summing up the day's rain of thought for a friend, we focus on what's of common interest, thus we extract portions from time, extract them like the sailors of Galicia pulled the spilled oil from Galician seas: with our hands

what you salvage

unforgettable

excluded from the law because her existence can't be sacrificed but, yes, is subject to murder

any biopolitical community (all Galicia, you and me and what we drink in through our eyes) is a *lager*

The mountains blaze, block, turn the sun into an ingot of burnished gold / inside the mother and in lovers, becoming nutrients

nothing to do with *preciousness*, the poem, the architecture of branches, the ancient meadow, are an authentic hall of wonders in the world (a fragment of *terra firma*, a spiral trumpet . . .), the dream of Terror, a beast, consanguineous, they erase the name (my name)

that's when Mariana (angel) abandons quietude

if revolution blazes, if like the syllable it can't die, if no ideology can really adhere to it . . . ?

what we see is its consistency

a distance in language-years
because of this, when we listen to the dead speak, their voice preserved on audiomagnetic tape, or when we hear a language whose meaning we don't know, the words are like the vision of the walls of Jericho falling, like the wee bird that sang to Ero at Armenteira[1]. That voice can be transported into the poem

that voice is the poem

**

True, the voice of the animal can't be written down
but that non-word returns
comes back
and repeats itself
that voice was *I*

that morpheme of blood

and you who always talk to me
now we both lower our gaze to those green tiles just like the airport tiles in the country where it always rains, and as if on a moving sidewalk we go from room to room and back to the operations centre where, as in aerodromes, only bodies matter, names of bodies and their histories. The author you quote speaks of seven gestures that produce nation: birth, emergency, initiative, post-position, sense of theatrical practice, linguistic transmission and absolution . . . thus you realize that you write in the language of your forebears so as to absolve yourself of the suffocating bonds of our particular identity project, and in this language you can reach—you claim—a road to non-knowledge that surpasses the violence tied to the linguistic conflict of origin

absolution in the face of the historical catastrophes of nation and of the language proper to it, this sense of moral failure, etc.

we waste so much time in self-loathing that we end up not knowing what brings favourable winds and what doesn't

and you can ponder it endlessly, ask yourself yet again if you should welcome the next words or not, these words that confess themselves; the poem dotes on tiny portions of ecstasy or existence and every affect

or continue shaping a "lyric" that abstracts itself, indifferent to what happens, to what happens to us

and return to the inarticulate sounds of pleasure, to that instant of silence, when you're born but air has yet to burst into the lungs, to the exclamatory voice that precedes pain and death

it holds so much, keeps coursing

the voice of metal, murmur of the ether

or, as the author of your text suggests, birth not into a language
but into the great poems of languages, into the Galician poetry of
Curros, Pondal, Rosalía

as when a cave lights up and sings
when caves sing

how would it be then, our being-there?

***

speech spoken by tyrants, victims, literary figures never stop
speaking, actresses speak in the theatre, gravediggers, wives, we
speak and don't stop speaking

but *I* doesn't speak

those who speak are the same ones who can't speak

rivers, meteors, mountains

in the flagstones the symbolic coats of arms, the animal horde or
in the great hydraulic empires

(here deer appear, cross in front of the car—I love life, life with
you, the life we share and we've still a year left, or all the years in the
world; but a poet, a poet can't explain, fully, what s/he writes; no
human can; in this sense we're all prisoners in some concentration
camp. In all, what I wanted to tell you is that somehow in the
voice, in the voice we articulate when we speak . . . no, it's not easy
but yes, yes we can perceive those remains, the rubble of a distinct

voice, different, earlier sounds, prior to speech, and meditating on these indications, searching out some illustrative image, I remembered cave paintings and with total clarity the Assyrian bas-relief 'The Dying Lion' in the hunts of Ashurbanipal, and I thought that the braying of that lioness could only be composed with desert colours)

and the skin a thousand kisses for Lesbia

as many as grains of sand
as many as deserts

deep and outside is the liver, womb, lightning

With you
with all peoples and all languages and all the living and the dead

Earth
subject
and sovereignty

Here life, here death.

**

maybe her greatest act of reason was a sketch of erotic fantasies, a narrative and iconic formula that led her to the ecstasy of the senses

the name of that abstraction is blind, winged and armed.

You and me
our way of relating has no voice

transparent as a carbon atom, voiceless
the blank voice of spelling

inside, we're no different than the stars

asteroid after asteroid after asteroid after asteroid

than the colossal elephant or languid giraffe

you don't see her?
she's coming
with six personal pronouns

you and I
(author-she / reader, s/he)
grapple with death

*

certain locations near the seamounts, where no sun is needed in
order to sing

Spring is slow, we all find it hard to burst into leaf

each tunnel that opens is worth life to us
each millimetre is truth

so we abandon the Vistula and head inland on a highway past bare
trees dotted with blackbird nests

the toilets are downstairs
tiny windows as in a train station

I don't know why / in my dreams it's drawn in italic capital letters,
or maybe it's the middle word that bends with the arch; they aren't
italics at all: square, stark and absolutely clear

our walk turns incredulous, slow, somnambulant

you can't really tell what you're seeing, you're facing a tangle or
trickles of steel, shaped like the crown of a tree with eyeglasses in
it, and you remember an afternoon long ago, in the Tate, in front
of some Rothkos; but the eyeglasses are really here, some still have
lenses, others only frames

thousands of pairs of shoes, thousands of suitcases, clothes,
toothbrushes, shaving brushes, cans of shoe polish

you stumble, you aren't really walking properly, you keep crashing
into display windows, of incalculable proportions . . . suitcases:
names, *the tiny handwriting of people who still believed in light*

and it's as if your eyes split from you or your gaze moves at triple
speed: at the same time in your visual field are Valentí, orthopedics
and the entry to the warehouse of hair; you search for blue, you
listen to birdsong and in a flash you face disconnection, lettering

the moment suspended
eternal

you repeat / you're across from the worn boots, facing the vials of
cyanide
you insist

and you come upon tiny clothes, photos of children, of the
children of Auschwitz and you're eyeless, like everyone else in this
state museum of Oświęcim

in lake country, in mosquito swampland, in marshes

in the cellblocks, the sense of sight is already gone from you, you
slowly touch your hand to the bricks, because they lead you to
windows, to this—so-called—"execution wall," and you force
yourself to break free and to move and there's no horror, only
surrender, a domination of reason

and you don't lean on anything you don't fall over, you follow the
example of the trees

you follow a rhythm, a route, no, no, you can't freeze up here

you evaluate proportions, details

………………………………..

I often think that if I had to peel everything away and define
myself I'd say: I'm a woman who twice gave birth, who dressed the
corpse of her biological father, who faced the canisters, the worn
canisters, who faced letters, lettering, the worn letters Zyklon-B,
and who read that word with difficulty

all that I write is the rubble of a literally razed poetics, signs of a muse without attributes / I don't feel even nostalgia

language is as dense as resin

imprisoned, interned, the flesh pours these words

language is of gold
the leaf that opens now on the willow

an ellipse in filigree completely spread that, in itself and in translation, breaks

This journey starts with a letter I never managed to write. My shadow waited for some pharaoh to emerge from stone and expected to agree on a dialogue with you. In all, no directive from History would reach me, I'd already be on the far side of the abyss, as abstraction and difference

and I'd return again and again to the figure of the *musulman* in the camps

to that double exclusion, from the animal and from the logos

it's a gaze without borders

even though the body cedes to death, it fights back when reason is being exhausted

it means that the heart must weigh the same as—or a bit less than—the plume of Osiris

*

at night, the pallor and relief of the white clover flower or *trifolium repens* make the fields visible, perforate the fields.

Of this scene, I'll just tell you:
in the vestibule, wide and bright after the renovations, I introduced María, Ana, Marta and Iria to Paco; the women walked toward us from the toilets. For a moment it was like the photo of my mother and her friends in 1952: they were intelligence and beauty and the possibility or impossibility of reproduction of the species. They appeared again to me, fleetingly, eternal.

What matters isn't what I could feel, but the real existence of the house and that dreams resided there; most are chapters, sections of novels: some hard-to-solve murder, shots fired by the vice-consul in Lahore, Lowry's volcanoes . . . unfold like atmospheric phenomena, all-encompassing, and despite belonging to literature they emit no sound but luminous epiphanies of pure pigmentation like the installations of Anish Kapoor

when I arrived I hoped to find my sister and brother comrades. No, the house isn't abandoned, between us everything was a cyclone of blood and totem

there are other ways of seeing it, of course

*

if in the building I'll never meet my brothers and sisters of influence, if I can enter and leave, cope with its antarctic desolation, if I know its dreams, what's next?

if I can access what is generated when the construction shuts its eyes, am I this house?

but when I recognized the dreams I was nearby, on the outskirts I investigate and expose the map's clandestine direction

as a young woman I went out repeatedly with a man to watch Sam Peckinpah movies. I detested those movies

the clandestine direction comes when the executioners decide

of conjugal union for example

clearly the poem isn't going to reveal the hidden action of its cells

that burst in the skies like northern lights

or atomic fission

**

despite this, night sky still worries me

if I substitute the astral figures that I trace in imaginary lines guided by cave paintings, and with the present in turn guiding the cave animals / I project the copulation of the ancestors in incessant transformation, so that dreams would be Hades and all nocturnal initiations a shamanic voyage

what bursts is the animal, its loss is language
it breaks in the skies and in the void, in the eyes, when the eyes see inside the eyes
it erupts in greenery

from cave to sky and from sky to cave, from cave to womb

we call it spring

***

whoever sleeps transforms into Eden and shadow, contemplates their dismembering, the excrement that anoints the word. (star)

just as the mother, assuming the baby understands, talks to it, so the poem addresses us

from womb to womb, in each and all the women ancestors, when only the heart's rhythm was known and the lungs hadn't yet been torn by air

long before your birth, it's your sky of diamonds

I write

****

when we dream, the stopovers in trembling and abrupt transformation are always spring and winter. Persephone dissects Hades

to evoke the garden, luminosity in the plenitude of winter / not only Eurydice but the genitals tauten, the couple encircled by the species, brutally outside the logos

every night, when language shuts its eyes, it descends to the depths. There, by a placid river, in a forest, the body of Orpheus is dismembered by ecstasy

the screen on which we project ourselves is as blurry as the waters; inside the drum, animals live, ancestors that mate and dream of spring and every night the voice we learn fascinated from the mother is shattered by drunken copulation

it's Eurydice and Orpheus who point out North, polarization, stars. They disperse the social, the mother tongue, cavort in a garden, copulate

*

yesterday, an algae green and thick in the current was cobra, drakar, a laugh of animality, Medusa, Orpheus, Eurydice

No, paradise is not childhood, paradise is animality; it's the paradise we've lost

green light, liquid / of oaks, river waters and the body in the current
they fold (waters, light)
nutritious

for a whole summer, hidden on the balcony in the noon heat, I tried to read *The Amazing Adventures of Captain Antifer*, I traced intrinsic and imaginary routes on the table, learned calm, the concentration that envelops work, the separation from the world

that's how an arm turns itself into rhythm

we hardly have any ruins, all our former agrarian production is a ruin but no one describes the fields as "ruined": if we had ruins we'd have memory
I have a head full of ruins

on the ruin you can clearly see History's profile

the ruin is a blur
we open a mineral vein in it, a sluice in its entrails

a pretty myth between flesh and word
a myth *I*
memory, instant, and immediately ruin

we're all (women ancestors) pretty much identical
we feel the voice thunder in the diaphragm, the lightning of thought in the dome

simians, they dilate the mind
and you, who love me.

Fog (the dog) kept straining at being unable to hunt and the
squirrels went stock-still and indiscernible in the woods, later she
(the dog) headed to a meadow, once in awhile one of the horses
spooked the flies and for a moment they buzzed in confusion then
landed cozily in their favourite spots

like this emptiness, Hölderlin tower
you who receive me

Babylon.

2

thus the poem, a blood that keeps the dead on the other border,
everything attracts it

myth—like the I, memory, fracture, time, copulation and dream—
unifies the unprecedented

towards an enamelled blue door where the animals are gods and
implode.

That incision is memory
an underwater path, worn pebbles, all the ochres of a river
or mud that rises with the blood when you step in it

from the air Galicia is a place where vegetation and crops are
mattresses or carpets of various sizes; you feel if you threw yourself
down you'd just float up again in a process of victory over gravity,
really you could live with this protective cushion for the rest of
your days

which is why the people who opted for primal variety must be
gymnasts and acrobats

Galicia from the sky is a system of immunitary comfort

the gestation of a book is a pregnancy of unpredictable length; its
later publication an invitation into light, into air, into the time
when a poem has to stand on its own

all this generally follows the collapse of the Milky Way

and no, I hardly slept because the police commissioner moved the
vegetable garden into the house and with it the trees and with the
trees the birds

persons are ramparts of insurmountable respect

then came fascism and for this reason no one wrote a novel like
Berlin Alexanderplatz or *Manhattan Transfer* in my language and
don't come back to me saying that in my language there's no city
like Dublin

it's difficult but you can figure it out

it's not that the *I* constitutes itself in the poem, but that the poem is an animation, so women seem crazy, what happens to us is existence

my political heart, well obviously I'd rather not wake up with so much resentment

destruction in Galicia doesn't involve the inorganic, so we can't say we had ruins; destruction in Galicia relates to disarticulation of the social fabric and of moral parameters, thus we can't lay claim to ruins (linguistic ruins, the ruins of productive mental units can't be assessed). In other countries, destruction also involves the inorganic (bombings). We can't claim that a heart attack is a ruin of the heart, a ruined heart

a heart's not an inorganic muscle

and the devices of writing collapse into a scribble and the flimsy and hypothetical themes of future thinking

it doesn't seem that clouds navigate in a hostile medium

if it isn't a war, who's shooting, who's killing you, who's the enemy?

The war we lost wasn't atomic but wasn't conventional either. The despotism of that oligarchy lasted forty years

that cells migrate doesn't mean they move; when an embrionary gland settles in its adult location, some cells, archaic, live on and share the fate of the tissue

of an animal we could say: its whole body is a technology

authors from the past create order in my syntax, I don't have much to do: I work on cutting a deal with time, so Kronos will grant me an intelligent fissure

if you write, words yield, you practice incisions, they're circuits of equilibrium

to follow the course of the Milky Way is to reach the end of Earth

but they search for the pulse of the magnificent

they insist

they go toward comrades of their generation dead on battlefields, in jails, in sites of extermination and exile

in the scenes of war that persist, that persist

Antonio's vanished body can be filled with any kind of fiction, the fable of his relationship with me opens every type of possibility

we're born

right in front of you, mothers of the horde
primates who bear in you the implant of the future and the standing stones (post-neolithic? yes, yes, pre-paleolithic, post-

neolithic)

contemporary

an instant

*

maybe this is why patriarchy sees human females as close to animality, meanwhile (generating and feeding the species) the flesh is congenial and indifferent to any prosthesis or technology

the caesura situates persons in opposite hemispheres. On one side we'd locate women, men and territories where we live under overlords of mediatized productivity, on the other, those with optimal access to the hand-brain conjunction

domestic animality of persons and territories justifies their exclusion from the bill of rights
this is an operative viewpoint, affects most humans and ecosystems, is called imperial biofascism.

Just as one fine day we can't open the strongbox with the usual combination, so when a book is shut, I the author, deambulate with all the excluded poems in a kind of limbo of expulsion and with a cardboard box, just one, to safeguard the clarity of dreams

if this keeps up, one day I'll hear all the doors slam shut, one after another behind me

that you exist facilitates perfection in the tasks at hand

no, what you see's not a birch forest, it's masses of white butterflies caught in the fat of trees; you see the bones of ancestors and of innumerable domestic animals that died with them, fulgurant in permafrost

The abyss was solid and surrounded the cooking fire with a cone/ whose verdure was nocturnal and skies/ ashgrey and blue, a promise

the key was the narrow path, full of snow and ice; I thought maybe I could crawl along the edges by grabbing onto lichen, root, or small weeds

one of the centaurs let me know that not he nor any of the others (centaurs) would be responsible for my life; soon dogs started barking and the skies fell on us

the quadrupeds were sleeping curled up, belly inward, and clearly I was scared but rested under the viscera of the horses

at dawn the mares stood up and first fog then rain settled into the mountains.

**

For three months now she's been writing her death and no, it can't be said that "death was implanted in her embryo" but rather "they grew up together / in a womb"

my skin, my eyes, my intelligence

they probably attended different schools: She didn't sense it, or didn't know how to name what she sensed . . . she'd go to a place where they'd teach her to handle / threads and breaths /

at first she thought "a nest of dark vegetation where a dream can sleep (almost-eternal) as far as possible from the logos" she took note of it

your skin, my eyes, your intelligence

on the day of the dead she was relieved to see the jack o'lantern
of the second-floor kid reflected in a balcony window and she
remembered carrying baby Atropos in her arms, protected by
darkness, as in a La Tour painting

clouds insist, but She only knows that clouds are made of water
and when the drops are heavy, they precipitate themselves, and
later she'll even be able to understand this, right now she doesn't
know why hot air has more humidity than polar air

fear is an accusatory finger, a blame, a judgement

Elizabeth, in a very calm voice, tells her that all the houses of her
life are at peace

she'd get there by plunging her gaze into the pages of sky, black
and fulgurant

to accept this intimate combustion

To respond is to harbour words:

I recall that very sky,	*With you I see these skies,*
and those gentle dawns above,	*I see these pale dawns,*
and those green fields that lie,	*I see these fields in flower*
with their coo of turtledoves	*Where coo the doves*

Janiwa. Janiw awitul quqanakäkiti, janiw janq'u pilpintunakäkisa,
janirakiw ch'akhäkisa. ¡Janiw ukamäkiti! (*Uñjasaw uñjtw
sañaxa, jan uñjasax janiw uñjtw sañäkiti*). Ukaw thakhixa,
juyphins qaqawarans wara waranakan thakhipax uksar aksar pallq

83

pallqawa, ¡ukhamaw thakhixa!

Bien sûr! Ni bouleaux ni papillons blancs ni l'os—(si l'on vient on peut dire qu'on a vu, si on ne vient pas, non—ils sont des chemins, des intersections d'étoiles, dans le givre.

To be compatible is to build a shelter; if it were a nest, we'd be birds

I don't know what great mountain or Pacific bird I'd want to be; a parakeet, an eaglet?
I could ask to be Morgana

a raven.

She keeps on the cloud path, perhaps because they're weightless (path, clouds) and balance each other like love and its canopy / wandering. White, purple or golden like lichen on rock

and they're a screen for blue and a screen for darkness

propulsed and free like everything that concentrates time

"we women dreamers are centaurs, but we don't share centaur dreams: we're centaur because our bodies are mammal but what we deduce is human. A centaur is a border figure, has the advantage of being able to walk on both sides but they're not reliable and awaken suspicion, are often castigated like Tiresias. We poems are centaurs, can placate wild beasts and move humans. If no dreamer underwrites your life it means no one will back up your integrity or support your requests. The poem is the one that rules the beasts, you can sleep with horses because they don't know what you dream"

so there are two kinds of centaur, poem centaurs and dreaming women centaurs: all are foundational and myths

a poet remembers, still remembers, still

thus *I* felt a huge exhaustion, not a sad exhaustion, *I* was a river and recalling who was coiled in a spiral made itself a nest; a nest is made with twigs and effort and into it plunge eagles, trout, lamprey and the salmon of a thousand rivers and all the dragonflies, earwigs, and all the summer butterflies and insects, and all the clouds reflected in the waters

I was dragon and remembering all the dragons of the most ancient massif altered them into a site of serenity and protection, to be able to think, which is a way to feel pleasure, will and distress

and they dangled themselves from trees and from the eaves of
houses

and a beautiful fishmonger walked by and she told them
"I'm going to the Mekong
I'm off to the Zambezi"

(and the reader to the author, she who is an infinity or two)
—you're writing a chronicle?
—ummm!
—but are we safe?
—yes, if it's an epic, we women are safe

but what about the beasts, the stones, the Thracian warriors!

Note (page 63)

[1] *Saint Ero*: Galician noble who founded a monastery at Armenteira in 1149, his story is one of the many Celtic chronicles of paradise. As abbot, he prayed every day to be shown Paradise. One day, walking near the monastery, Ero was dumbstruck by the song of a nightingale, and sat under an oak, savouring the sounds of the birdsong, and fell asleep. On his return to the monastery, the abbot hardly recognized the path, and was surprised at the changes to the monastery, for it was bigger, more modern, more monks. These monks find their oldest comrade who had heard about Abbot Ero in his youth, and he showed them a book that said Ero had vanished 300 years ago when he went to climb the mountain. Realizing he had been shown paradise, and in gratitude and amazement, Ero fell dead.

Hordes of Writing, the ninth book of poetry by the celebrated Galician writer Chus Pato, received the Spanish National Critics' Prize in 2008 and the Losada Diéguez Prize for Literature in Galicia in 2009. It is the third book of her poetry (with *m-Talá* and *Charenton*, both published by Shearsman Books and BuschekBooks) to appear in English translation. Pato has performed from her work in England, Wales, Ireland, Poland, Germany, France, Spain, Portugal, Morocco, Argentina, Chile, Cuba and Canada, among others. She lives and works in Lalín, Galicia, Spain, where she teaches geography and history.

§

Chus Pato's translator, Erín Moure, is a poet and translator from French, Galician, Spanish and Portuguese into English. She lives and works in Montréal, Québec. Her most recent book is *O Resplandor*. She is currently translating Pato's *Secession*.

CPSIA information can be obtained at www.ICGtesting.com
Printed in the USA
LVOW121835230812

295668LV00004B/195/P